COVER: "THE FOOTBALL PLAYERS"
LES JOUEURS DE FOOTBALL, 1908

THE FOOTBALL PLAYERS, WEARING COLORFUL COSTUMES, ARE ALL IN MOTION EXCEPT THE SAFETY MAN. HE STANDS READY FOR ACTION.

SOLOMON R. GUGGENHEIM MUSEUM, NEW YORK

THIS CIRCLE OF PLAYERS KEEPS OUR ATTENTION CONSTANTLY MOVING AROUND THE PAINTING. THE PLAYERS ARE BORDERED BY AN AUDIENCE OF AUTUMN-COLORED TREES. IN FRANCE, AS IN THE UNITED STATES, THIS IS THE FOOTBALL SEASON. THE LEAVES RESEMBLE THOUSANDS OF APPLAUDING HANDS.

AT THE CENTER OF THE SCENE, ALONG THE HORIZON, FOUR TREES STRETCH THEIR NECKS INTO THE CLOUDS AS IF TO SEE THE GAME.

DETAIL FROM "THE MUSE INSPIRING THE POET"

THE MUSE INSPIRING THE POET , 1909   KUNSTMUSEUM , BASEL , PUBLIC ART COL.   COLORPHOTO HINZ , BASEL

DEDICATED TO BRADLEY SMITH, HIS CHILDREN AND HIS CHILDREN'S
CHILDREN

LIBRARY OF CONGRESS CATALOGING-IN-PUBLICATION DATA
RABOFF, ERNEST LLOYD
    HENRI ROUSSEAU
    (ART FOR CHILDREN)
REPRINT. ORIGINALLY PUBLISHED: GARDEN CITY, N.Y.: DOUBLEDAY, 1970. SUMMARY: A BRIEF BIOGRAPHY OF HENRI ROUSSEAU ACCOMPANIES FIFTEEN COLOR
REPRODUCTIONS AND CRITICAL INTERPRETATIONS OF HIS WORKS. 1. ROUSSEAU, HENRI JULIEN FÉLIX, 1844-1910-JUVENILE LITERATURE. 2. PAINTERS-
FRANCE-BIOGRAPHY-JUVENILE LITERATURE. 3. PRIMITIVISM IN ART-FRANCE-JUVENILE LITERATURE. 4. ROUSSEAU, HENRI JULIEN FÉLIX, 1844-1910-
CRITICISM AND INTERPRETATION-JUVENILE LITERATURE. 5. PAINTING, FRENCH-JUVENILE LITERATURE. 6. PAINTING, MODERN-19TH CENTURY-FRANCE-
JUVENILE LITERATURE. 7. PAINTING, MODERN-20TH CENTURY-FRANCE-JUVENILE LITERATURE. [1. ROUSSEAU, HENRI JULIEN FÉLIX, 1844-1910. 2. ARTISTS.
3. PAINTING, FRENCH. 4. PAINTING, MODERN. 5. ART APPRECIATION] I. ROUSSEAU, HENRI JULIEN FÉLIX, 1844-1910. II. TITLE. III. SERIES: ART FOR CHILDREN.
ND553.R67R3   1988   759.4   [92]   87-16862   ISBN 0-397-32221-6
    "A HARPER TROPHY BOOK"   ISBN 0-06-446069-X(PBK.)   87-17700

HENRI ROUSSEAU

By Ernest Raboff

ART
FOR
CHILDREN

A HARPER TROPHY BOOK

HARPER & ROW, PUBLISHERS

HENRI ROUSSEAU (ON-REE' RU-SO'), CALLED 'DOUANIER', WAS BORN IN LAVAL, FRANCE, IN 1844.

AFTER A SHORT TIME IN THE FRENCH ARMY HE WAS MARRIED TO CLÉMENCE BOITARD. FOR THE NEXT TWENTY YEARS HE WORKED AS A TOLL COLLECTOR "DOUANIER" BUT ALSO FOUND TIME TO PAINT.

AT THE AGE OF FORTY HE RETIRED TO BECOME A FULL-TIME ARTIST. HE GAVE ART AND VIOLIN LESSONS FOR THE REST OF HIS LIFE AND WELCOMED ALL WHO CAME TO HIM — RICH OR POOR, FAMOUS OR UNKNOWN. HE DIED IN 1910.

ROUSSEAU

WAS A SELF-TAUGHT ARTIST WHO PAINTED WITH BOTH INWARD AND OUTWARD VISION. THESE BRIGHT VISIONS GLOW FOR US IN EVERY PAINTING.

DRAWING OF THE ARTIST BY RABOFF

HENRI ROUSSEAU WROTE POEMS, PLAYS AND MUSIC. SOMETIMES HE SANG HIS OWN SONGS. HIS POEMS AND HIS SONGS, LIKE HIS PAINTINGS, REVEAL A GENTLE HEART AND A VIVID IMAGINATION.

ROUSSEAU'S CLOSE FRIEND, THE ARTIST AND COLLECTOR ROBERT DELAUNAY, WROTE: "ROUSSEAU WAS VERY KIND AND HOSPITABLE. HE WAS HAPPY TO RECEIVE YOU EVEN WHEN HE HAD HIS PALETTE IN HAND. HE WOULD ASK YOU TO SIT DOWN AND KEEP ON WORKING. I WAS ATTRACTED BY HIS CALM, HIS DEEP SATISFACTION IN HIS WORK."

HENRI ROUSSEAU ONCE WROTE THAT ANY MAN WHOSE THOUGHTS ASPIRE TO BEAUTY AND GOOD SHOULD BE PERMITTED TO CREATE IN HIS OWN WAY, IN TOTAL FREEDOM.

MYSELF: PORTRAIT-LANDSCAPE (DETAIL)   NATIONAL GALLERY, PRAGUE

DETAIL

IN "SPRING IN THE VALLEY OF BIÈVRE" ROUSSEAU SHOWS US A VIEW OF A WINDY DAY IN WEST FRANCE. THE BRANCHES OF THE TREES INTERTWINE IN THE SPRING SKY AS THOUGH TO KEEP FROM BLOWING AWAY.

THE GREEN GRASS IS STRIPED BY TRAILS OF SUNLIGHT SLANTING THROUGH THE TREES.

THE VILLAGERS WALK ON THE SUN-PATHS, SEEKING WARMTH AGAINST THE COLD WIND.

BEYOND THE PICKET FENCE, WINTER TREES SURROUND THE HOUSES AND PROTECT THEM FROM THE WEATHER.

HENRI ROUSSEAU HAS BEEN CALLED "THE MASTER OF THE TREES." THE ARTIST GREATLY ENJOYED ALL OF NATURE AND HIS FEELING IS REVEALED BY EVERY BRANCH AND EVERY LEAF IN HIS PAINTINGS.

SPRING IN THE VALLEY OF BIÈVRE   THE METROPOLITAN MUSEUM OF ART, GIFT OF MARSHALL FIELD, 1939

DETAIL

"PAYSAGE EXOTIQUE"

SHOWS HOW ROUSSEAU'S VISITS TO THE BOTANICAL GARDENS AND THE ZOOS OF PARIS STIMULATED HIS COLORFUL IMAGINATION. AFTER THESE VISITS HE WOULD CREATE HIS OWN JUNGLES, SOMETIMES PAINTING INTO THEM ANIMALS THAT MAY NEVER HAVE EXISTED AND INVENTING TREES AND FLOWERS.

ROUSSEAU STUDIED ANIMALS, CHILDREN, PLANTS AND FLOWERS BUT LIKE ALL GREAT ARTISTS, HE GAVE THEM A FRESH NEW IDENTITY.

HIS ORANGES BECAME LIKE SUNS... HIS LEAVES AND FLOWERS LIKE BIRDS... AND HIS MONKEYS, AS IN THIS PAINTING, BECAME LIKE PLAYING CHILDREN.

PAYSAGE EXOTIQUE   MRS. ROBERT R. MC CORMICK COLLECTION, WASHINGTON, D.C.

"VASE OF FLOWERS" TELLS A GREAT DEAL ABOUT THE ARTISTIC FEELINGS OF ROUSSEAU. EACH SINGLE FLOWER AND LEAF, EACH PETAL AND BUD IS CAREFULLY AND PAINSTAKINGLY PAINTED. EACH HAS AN INDIVIDUAL PERSONALITY, ITS OWN LINES AND FORMS, AS DOES EACH OF THE FINGERS ON OUR HANDS.

DETAIL

HENRI ROUSSEAU BELIEVED THAT ALL FORMS OF LIFE WERE EQUALLY VALUABLE. FLOWERS AND TREES WERE AS IMPORTANT TO HIM AS WERE ANIMALS AND PEOPLE.

AROUND THE VASE OF FLOWERS ROUSSEAU BRINGS THE SUNLIGHT INDOORS WITH THE BRIGHT ORANGE TABLECLOTH. AND THOUGH THE PAINTING IS MAINLY OF FLOWERS, HE FOUND A PLACE FOR HIS FAVORITE SUBJECT, TREES. THEIR FIVE-POINTED LEAVES, LIKE HANDPRINTS, DECORATE THE SMOOTH TABLECLOTH.

VASE OF FLOWERS   MR. AND MRS. WILLIAM S. PALEY COLLECTION , NEW YORK

"TOLL HOUSE" IS A PAINTING OF ONE OF THE MANY CUSTOMHOUSES WHERE TAXES WERE COLLECTED FROM FARMERS AND MERCHANTS AS THEY BROUGHT THEIR PRODUCTS INTO PARIS TO SELL. THIS MAY BE THE VERY TOLL HOUSE WHERE ROUSSEAU WORKED FOR TWENTY YEARS.

THERE IS BOTH PEACE AND DISCIPLINE IN THE PICTURE. THE GUARDS STAND VERY STIFFLY, AND THE ONE ON THE ROOF CAN OBSERVE THINGS THAT THE GUARD ON THE GROUND CANNOT SEE. EVEN THE TREES, THE TWO CHIMNEYS AND THE STEEPLE STAND LIKE SENTINELS.

IT IS A CALM, QUIET SCENE. FOR THIS ARTIST IT WAS THE PERFECT JOB. IT GAVE HIM TIME TO IMAGINE FARAWAY SCENES THAT HE COULD LATER PUT INTO HIS PAINTINGS. FOR THOUSANDS OF HOURS STRETCHING OVER A PERIOD OF TWENTY YEARS HE MADE DRAWINGS AND THOUGHT ABOUT HIS TREES, FLOWERS, PEOPLE AND ANIMALS.

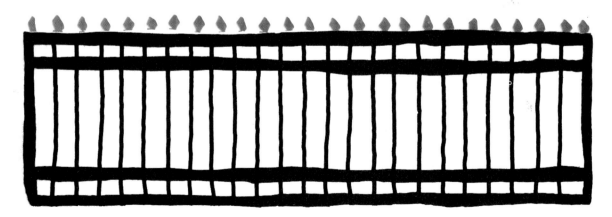

THE TOLL HOUSE   COURTAULD INSTITUTE GALLERIES, LONDON UNIVERSITY

NOTRE DAME, ONE OF THE WORLD'S MOST FAMOUS CATHEDRALS, HAS BEEN PAINTED BY NEARLY EVERY ARTIST WHO HAS LIVED IN PARIS. IN THIS PAINTING ROUSSEAU HAS PICTURED THIS GRACEFUL CHURCH AS A PART OF THE CITY'S DAILY LIFE. WE EXPLORE THE ANCIENT BRIDGE CURVING OVER THE RIVER SEINE, THE DARK HOUSE BOAT, THE BUILDINGS LOOMING LIKE CLIFFS WITH HUNDREDS OF EYES WATCHING OVER THE LEAFY TREE-LINED RIVER BANKS AND THE CITY'S PEOPLE WHO PAUSE OR PASS THERE.

BY READING A PAINTING SLOWLY, LIKE A POEM OR A BOOK, WE CAN RECEIVE MUCH PLEASURE AS DETAILS OF THE PICTURE RECALL HAPPY SCENES FROM OUR OWN STORE OF MEMORIES.

ROUSSEAU, WHO PAINTED NATURE SO LOVINGLY AND CLEARLY, CAN VISUALLY RECALL THESE PLEASURES FOR ALMOST ANYONE WHO ENJOYS THE OUT-OF-DOORS TAKE TIME TO ENJOY THE NOTRE DAME OF PARIS.

DETAIL

NOTRE DAME THE PHILLIPS COLLECTION, WASHINGTON, D.C.

IN PORTRAIT OF A YOUNG GIRL ROUSSEAU,
LIKE OTHER UNSCHOOLED OR "PRIMITIVE" ARTISTS, MAKES
EVERY BRUSH STROKE AN EXCITING PART OF THE PAINTING.
IN LOOKING CLOSELY AT THE DETAILS OF THIS WOODLAND
PORTRAIT THE BACKGROUND MAY REMIND US OF THE
MIRACLE OF A TREE AND THE PLANNED DESIGN IN A LEAF.
THE GIRL'S GARMENT MAY MAKE US THINK OF THE LABOR
OF LOVE IN A HAND SEWN DRESS, HER LONG BLOND
HAIR OF A WATERFALL.

THE NINE TREES HEDGING THE WOODS STAND AS STRAIGHT
AS THE YOUNG GIRL. THEIR FLOWERING BRANCHES WIND
THROUGH EACH OTHER LIKE THE FLOWERS TWINED IN
THE TRESSES OF HER HAIR.

DETAIL

THE ARTIST HAS INCLUDED IN
THE PICTURE A WHITE LAMB
AND A BLACK LAMB. THE GIRL
SEEMS TO BE OFFERING A
BRANCH OF LEAVES TO THE
BLACK ONE. ROUSSEAU, WHO
WAS OFTEN ALONE, PERHAPS
UNDERSTOOD BLACK SHEEP.
HE MAY BE SAYING THAT WE
ARE ALL LAMBS IN THE
FOREST OF LIFE AND WE MUST
BE KIND TO ONE ANOTHER.

PORTRAIT OF A YOUNG GIRL, 1893-95   PHILADELPHIA MUSEUM OF ART COLLECTION

"THE SLEEPING GYPSY"
WAS DESCRIBED AS FOLLOWS
BY ROUSSEAU IN A LETTER:

"A WANDERING GYPSY WHO
PLAYS THE MANDOLIN, WITH
HER JAR NEXT TO HER (A
VASE CONTAINING DRINKING
WATER), IS DEEPLY ASLEEP,
WORN OUT FROM FATIGUE.
A LION HAPPENS BY, SNIFFS
AT HER, AND DOES NOT DEVOUR
HER. THERE IS AN EFFECT

DETAIL

OF MOONLIGHT, VERY POETIC. THE SCENE TAKES PLACE
IN A COMPLETELY ARID DESERT. THE GYPSY IS
DRESSED IN ORIENTAL FASHION."

HENRI ROUSSEAU, LIKE HIS GYPSY, WAS A MUSICIAN
WHO WANDERED THE STREETS OF PARIS PLAYING
HIS VIOLIN.

HE WOULD PLAY HIS MUSIC AND PAINT HIS PICTURES
UNTIL HE WAS TOO TIRED TO CONTINUE. THEN HE
WOULD LIE DOWN AND SLEEP BELIEVING THAT HIS LOVE
FOR NATURE AND FOR LIFE WOULD ALWAYS PROTECT
HIM FROM ANY HARM.

THE SLEEPING GYPSY, 1897   MUSEUM OF MODERN ART, NEW YORK, GIFT OF MRS. SIMON GUGGENHEIM

"HAPPY QUARTET"

IS ROUSSEAU'S VISION OF ADAM AND EVE
IN PARADISE.

FOR THIS ARTIST, A JOYFUL SCENE MUST CONTAIN A CHILD
AND AN ANIMAL TO BE A REAL GARDEN OF EDEN. HE COULD
NOT DREAM OF LIFE WITHOUT CHILDREN OR THEIR PETS.

IN THIS PAINTING, ADAM IS A MUSICIAN. HE PLAYS THE
FLUTE. EVE HOLDS A BEAUTIFUL GARLAND WOVEN OF
VINES, RED FLOWERS AND LEAVES.

THE LONG BLADES OF GRASS IN THE LEFT FOREGROUND
SEEM TO SWAY TO ADAM'S MELODY. THEIR FIRM,
STRAIGHT LINES HAVE MASCULINE STRENGTH. THE
YELLOW DOG POINTS HIS HEAD SKYWARD, PERHAPS
ADDING HIS VOICE TO THE MUSIC OF THE HAPPY QUARTET.
THE CHILD ROMPS WITH A GARLAND.

EVE HAS HER AUDIENCE TOO. AT HER SIDE, THE FULL
LEAVES OF THE PLANT HAVE ROUNDED, FEMININE
FORMS. ROUSSEAU HAS FILLED THE BILLOWING
TREES BEHIND THE QUARTET WITH
COLORFUL, ALMOST DANCING
LEAVES.

THE HAPPY QUARTET   MR. AND MRS. JOHN HAY WHITNEY, NEW YORK

"STREET IN BANLIEU" IS ANOTHER PAINTING IN WHICH ROUSSEAU SHOWS HIS APPRECIATION FOR THE TREES, THE LEAVES, THE CLOUDS AND THE SKY.

THE HOUSES ARE USED AS A STAGE SETTING FOR THE ARTIST'S PLAY. THEIR WHITE, BLACK AND GRAY WALLS MAKE A GOOD BACKGROUND FOR THE FRESH GREEN TREES AND BUSHES.

STARTING FROM THE WHITE-SHIRTED WORKER, WE CAN BEGIN TO EXPLORE THE PAINTING. HIS SHOVEL POINTS OUR EYES TO THE EDGE OF THE STREET, WHICH LEADS US TO THE TWIN TREES ON THE RIGHT. LIKE

TWO ARROWS THEY TAKE US OVER THE ROOFTOPS AND ALONG THE WHITE CLOUDS.

THE RED GABLES, THE CHIMNEYS, THE WINDOWS REFLECT-ING THE INTENSE BLUE SKY, THE UNUSUAL LEAVES AND THE LEAF-PATTERNED WALLS KEEP OUR EYES MOVING AROUND THE SCENE UNTIL WE FEEL VERY FAMILIAR WITH THE CHARACTER OF THIS PARTICULAR QUIET STREET IN BANLIEU.

STREET IN BANLIEU   A. MAX WEITZENHOFFER, JR

"THE WATERFALL" IS A GREAT FANTASY LANDSCAPE.
AT THE LEFT OF THE SCENE, ROUSSEAU'S TALL TROPICAL
TREE WITH ITS BROAD, HEART-SHAPED LEAVES BENDS
OUR ATTENTION TO THE WHITE ROCK-BOUND WATERFALL,
TO THE MEN AND THE TWO ANIMALS.

THE RED-LEAFED PLANT IS AN EXPLOSIVE BASE FOR ANOTHER
TREE THAT RISES ROCKET-LIKE WITH BOLD GREEN CONE
LEAVES.

HIDDEN IN THE MIDDLE OF THE JUNGLE, A GROUP
OF GREEN TEPEES WITH DECORATED TOPS ADDS A
NOTE OF HARMONY BETWEEN MAN AND NATURE.

ROUSSEAU'S FAVORITE COLOR GREEN DOMINATES THE
PICTURE. TO HIM IT IS THE COLOR OF LIFE. IN HIS

DETAIL

IMAGINARY COUNTRY IT IS
ALWAYS SPRING OR SUMMER.

GREEN LEAVES ARE
LIKE MUSICAL NOTES
PLACED ALONG THE
STAFF-BRANCHES OF NATURE
FOR ROUSSEAU
TO SOUND WITH HIS
BRUSHES ON CANVAS.

THE WATERFALL, 1910   THE ART INSTITUTE OF CHICAGO, HELEN BIRCH BARTLETT MEMORIAL COL.

"SAWMILL NEAR PARIS" IS A GENTLE, SOFT-TONED PAINTING. IT IS LIKE A LULLABY PLAYED TENDERLY ON A VIOLIN. IT WAS TO THIS MILL THAT ROUSSEAU'S BELOVED TREES WERE BROUGHT FROM THEIR BIRTHPLACE IN THE FORESTS.

DETAIL

THE TREES WOULD BEGIN NEW LIVES AS LUMBER FOR TABLES, CHAIRS, WALLS, PICTURE FRAMES AND A THOUSAND OTHER ITEMS USEFUL TO MAN.

PERHAPS A YOUNG TREE WOULD BECOME A WAGON FOR THE BOY WHO HOLDS A BRANCH WITH BLOSSOMS, OR PERHAPS A WOODEN RATTLE FOR THE BABY OR A ROCKING CHAIR FOR THE MOTHER. OVER THEIR HEADS A FLOWERING TREE SEEMS TO BE WAVING GOODBYE TO THE BARK-STRIPPED YELLOW LOGS.

BEYOND THE SAWMILL AND THE WOODS, THE METAL FRAME OF THE EIFFEL TOWER POINTS INTO THE SKY LIKE A MAN-MADE TREE.

SAWMILL NEAR PARIS,   1893-95   ART INSTITUTE OF CHICAGO, GIFT OF KATE L. BREWSTER

"LIBERTY INVITING THE ARTISTS TO EXHIBIT AT THE 22ND SALON DES INDÉPENDANTS" SHOWS US THE ARTISTS ARRIVING WITH THEIR WORKS AT THE EXHIBITION HALL IN PARIS.

EVERYONE WHO PAINTS IS INVITED. IT IS AN IMPORTANT DAY FOR THE ARTISTS. THEY COME FROM MANY FOREIGN LANDS AND THE BRIGHT FLAGS OF THESE COUNTRIES CROWN THE SCENE.

LIBERTY IS SHOWN AS AN ANGEL TRUMPETING A WELCOME.

ROUSSEAU'S BELOVED TREES PROVIDE SHADE FOR LONG LINES OF ARTISTS WHO WAIT ON BOTH SIDES OF THE ENTRANCE HOLDING PAINTINGS UNDER THEIR ARMS.

PAINTINGS THAT ARE TOO LARGE TO CARRY ARE LOADED ONTO CARTS. THE HORSE-DRAWN WAGONS ARE AT THE LEFT, THE HAND-PULLED ONES ON THE RIGHT. IN THE FOREGROUND A LION HOLDS BETWEEN HIS PAWS A LIST OF NAMES WITH ROUSSEAU'S NAME AND THOSE OF HIS FRIENDS UPON IT.

DETAIL

LIBERTY INVITING THE ARTISTS TO EXHIBIT AT THE 22ND SALON DES INDÉPENDANTS, 1906   PRIVATE COLLECTION

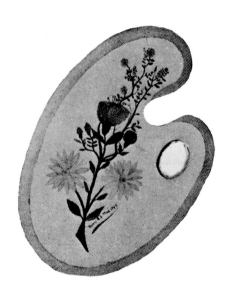

ROUSSEAU'S PALETTE, 1907